Surely if it be worth while troubling ourselves
about the works of art of today, of which any amount
almost can be done, since we are yet alive,
it is worth while spending a little care,
forethought and money preserving the art
of bygone ages, of which ... so little is
left, and of which we can never have
any more, whatever goodhap the
world may attain to.

William Morris 1881

Heritage Canada

Heritage Canada

photographs by Philip Graham

text by Martin Segger

McClelland and Stewart
and
The Heritage Canada Foundation

Art Direction & Design by Mary Ann Beckett Baxter.

Title calligraphy by Rita Edwards.

Photographs, copyright © 1981 by Philip Graham
Text, copyright © 1981 by Martin Segger

ALL RIGHTS RESERVED

ISBN 0-7710-3518-7

The Canadian Publishers
McClelland and Stewart Limited
25 Hollinger Road, Toronto M4B 3G2

Lithographed in Canada by Price Printing Ltd., Vancouver, B.C.

Produced by Canadian Heritage Publications Inc., © 1981.

W ithin the pages of this book, Canadians can glimpse the richness of their past — a past that was once thought of as dull and uninspiring and whose visual legacy has all too often been neglected or destroyed.

Philip Graham has been exploring that legacy and the results are here. The Heritage Canada Foundation, which helped to subsidize his cross-Canada Odyssey, is proud to sponsor this book. It gives the lie to those who still say there is nothing worth saving in this country and who continue to defend the destruction of our history in the name of progress.

The real progress in Canada has been the remarkable rise of the heritage preservation movement. Heritage Canada first came into being in 1972 as a private charitable foundation whose task was to give national impetus to a burgeoning grass roots movement. In those days, as I well remember, the idea of preserving *anything* was highly controversial. Even as we met for the first time as a board, the wreckers were destroying one of the most famous buildings in the country — the Montreal mansion of Sir William Van Horne, the man who built the Canadian Pacific Railway.

The past decade has been a remarkable about face in the attitude of the public, the politicians, and the real estate community toward the cultural landscape — the banks, churches, railway stations, private homes, public buildings, business blocks and main streets that act as living history lessons.

We at Heritage Canada cannot claim much of the credit for this change. Clearly, the government of the day sensed it when they endowed the Foundation. We have only ridden the crest of a wave of public opinion, forged, I believe, in the crucible of the 1967 Centennial and given new impetus by an energy crisis that makes the destruction of any serviceable building a minor scandal.

At best the Foundation can act as a catalyst to put the idea of preservation — financing demonstration projects, such as our conservation areas in several major cities; experimenting in the revitalization of main streets in smaller towns; training architects, builders, artisans and the general public in forgotten techniques, through our "University without Walls"; lobbying governments for tougher heritage legislation and better income tax laws (which, at present conspire against preservation); and helping to produce magazines, pamphlets, films and books like this one.

We have had our triumphs and defeats. Some of the buildings shown here — St. Andrew's "salt box", for instance, Annapolis Royal's Runciman House, the Cobourg Town Hall — were saved and restored with our help. Others — the Birks building in Vancouver, the Capitol Theatre in Saskatoon, and Queen Street asylum in Toronto — were lost forever in spite of our intervention.

It is important to remember that most of the buildings and artifacts shown here have been saved largely through the efforts of anonymous but dedicated Canadians. Given the new temper of the times, I think we can say that these, at least, are no longer in danger. This book demonstrates in the most graphic way why it was necessary to preserve them. For this is much more than a collection of pretty pictures of quaint or eccentric structures. It is a learning experience. Mr. Graham has so arranged and selected his photographs as to give all of us a new insight into our past and a new understanding of what it means to be a Canadian.

Pierre Berton

Pierre Berton
Chairman, Board of Governors
The Heritage Canada Foundation

Nations are, indeed, built. From the massive timbers hewn from virgin forests, boulders gathered from the untilled land, turf itself pried from the bald prairie, granite cut from precipitous cliffs and from bricks, first shipped as ballast in the sailing vessels which bore as cargo the cast iron, glass, and roofing slate later manufactured in local factories, our nearly four-hundred-year history is fashioned. From early hunting and gathering tribes through the first Europeans at Port Royal in 1605, from the traders and explorers to railroad builders and bush pilots, the Canadas have been peopled by travellers and builders. The temporary and ephemeral have been the hallmark of our history, the rule rather than the exception.

Early Newfoundland fishermen who attempted to establish a permanent foothold in the first windswept outports could expect to be periodically burnt out by anti-settlement fish traders. The *coureurs des bois* and, later, the factors of the great fur trading companies, established camps and forts along the great interior waterways, but these were maintained only so long as traffic and profit dictated. Then followed the nineteenth century entrepreneurial age. The boomtown false-front was intended only for show as long as the motherlode lasted. Even the cast iron columns and pressed tin cornices of roaring Toronto or booming Winnipeg were quickly fabricated to claim instant prosperity rather than long-term respectability.

Prairie settlers put up crude shelters hoping to express improvement and success with larger mansions as soon as possible. The towering matchwork trestles which carried the first trains of the Canadian Pacific Railway through the Rockies in the 1880s lasted only until better routes could be discovered or less arduous grades devised. Prefabricated, do-it-yourself houses, bank buildings, even churches, could be catalogue-ordered and transported to site by ship or railroad.

Travellers and builders, we are a nation which, by the very enterprise of our history, has inherited a life style that devalues or ignores permanent symbols of the past as anchor points for the future. Only recently have we begun to examine the humble ancestral home, the original plot of carefully planted shade trees, the masterfully crafted early community church, or the whimsical detail of an old commercial street front. Only slowly have we begun to appreciate that, while burdened with axes, trowels, and ploughs, the early settlers also carried an additional baggage of customs, ideals, and traditions. As well as illustrating skill, tenacity, and brute strength, the old homes, stores, churches, court houses and parliament buildings celebrate the visions prompted by a variety of cultures and ambitions.

Tsimshian bear pole carved by Mr. Charles Dudoward of Port Simpson Indian Band at Fort Simpson, B.C.

Hat Creek, British Columbia ➞

That this particular material record, our historical landscape, continues to speak for our pioneer ancestors must be a conscious choice of present and future Canadians. Already, throughout this country, that choice is being made. Enthusiasts restore old cars; bankers, bureaucrats and tradesmen buy and restore old houses; Toronto and Victoria decide to preserve their old city halls; local amenity societies press for the conservation of a nineteenth-century streetscape or an old mill; historical societies and all levels of government create heritage villages as educational memorials to early community enterprise.

The first step in preservation is to learn the vocabulary of the landscape, the marks, constructs, erasures and passages of history upon it. Here the selective frame and deliberate focus of the camera can be both guide and translator.

Necessity and economy dictated simple, severe building forms like these located at Upper Canada Village, Morrisburg, Ontario.

Canadian museums are renowned for their role in memorializing pioneer settlement life. The heritage village, based on the Scandinavian open-air museum movement of the late nineteenth century, thrives in Canada. More Canadians travel to historic sites every year than attend any other kind of recreational activity. The famous Upper Canada Village at Morrisburg, Ontario is a museum of buildings and artifacts gathered from the areas threatened by the creation of the St. Lawrence Seaway. Grouped together on a single site these structures illustrate Upper Canada's social and industrial history. The preserved gold-mining settlement of Barkerville in central British Columbia is a frozen moment in an actual 1870s boomtown. Fortress Louisburg in Nova Scotia is a total recreation from original plans, drawings, and written records. All these sites entertain, stimulate, and educate the visitor through appropriate artifacts and animation. Guides and craftsmen, often in period costume, explain and demonstrate historic ways of life.

Historic House museums such as the 1815 R. J. Uniacke home in Nova Scotia, or Craigflower Manor of 1856 in Victoria, document the life and times of former prominent citizens. In such cases the story of the family, based on personal papers and the course of local politics and commerce, is portrayed by the style of house, its furnishings and decoration.

National historic parks, in a chain of meticulous restorations starting at Fort Langley, B.C., then, crossing the country to Fort James, Rocky Mountain House, Lower Fort Garry and the isolated but preserved York Factory, link the country, celebrating the major centres of the all-important fur trade.

Militarism is not a dominant theme in Canadian history, yet such structures as Fort Henry at Kingston, Ontario are grim reminders of the age-old call to arms.

The dinner table awaits the family at the restored O'Keefe Ranch house near Vernon, British Columbia. ➤

Last whiskey finished, Barkerville, British Columbia. The chair is a "Cariboo Tipper".

Upper Canada Village, Morrisburg, Ontario

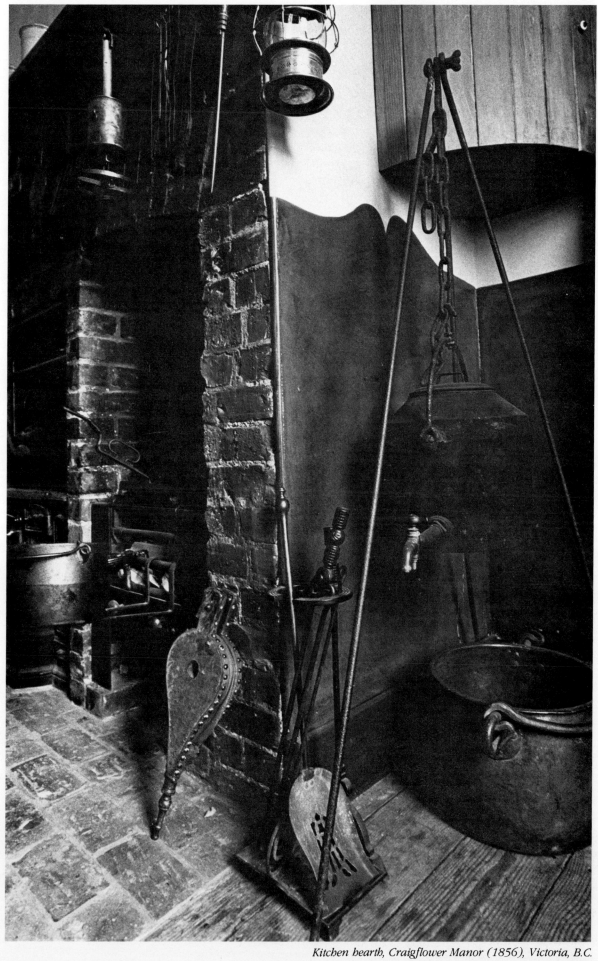

Kitchen hearth, Craigflower Manor (1856), Victoria, B.C.

First on the land meant first to construct a habitation. Forts, huts, barns, or grist mills then had to be fabricated from the materials and skills at hand. This was as true of the sixteenth-century French *habitant* as the twentieth-century Ukrainian immigrant. Throughout Canada a combination of factors — period of settlement, nationality of builder, unique resource of the locality — has created a wide variety of indigenous building traditions, lending each area its particular "sense of place."

In Eastern Canada these differences have deep roots. Medieval French building traditions came to New France with the *habitants* from areas such as Brittany and Normandy. The steep pitched roof with massive gable chimneys, the slightly hipped *coyau* (eaves to protect the walls), or its variant the *maison a croupe* (hipped pavilion roof) have survived in the St. Lawrence valley and are now being revived by

Quebec builders throughout this area and the Gaspe. The earliest structures of New France also copied the French building technology with the *colombage pierotte,* a rubble-filled, half-timber or field-stone masonry. This style soon gave way to a building technique better suited to the country's resources and climate, the now distinctive *piece-sur-piece* — large axe-squared timbers laid horizontally and slotted into vertical posts.

Upper Canada, a late eighteenth-century English creation, retains that architectural heritage through an indirect connection. The area's settlers were loyalist immigrants from the American breakaway colonies who brought with them severe symmetrical house forms with central entrance porches, clean-lined saddle roofs and non-expressive smooth stucco or clapboard exteriors. This style can be traced through late Victorian gothicised or Italianate versions to the present-day upright, two-storey box of the Ontario subdivision house. The eastern seaboard colonies have also retained an English Georgian ancestry, in particular the shingle-clad saltbox form, although here it is through the influence of their seventeenth-century New England neighbours. In eastern Nova Scotia and Prince Edward Island the influx of Scots has left its mark on the saltbox house type by adding the distinctive five-sided roof dormer. The domestic architecture of Newfoundland owes much to the same tradition, and similar lines of communication to the American seaboard. In St. John's and the outports however, contiguous classical street fronts, in smaller scale and with greater brevity of detail, are supplemented by Victorian variants of the same house type exhibiting a mansard second storey.

Ashton, Ontario

Kingston, Ontario

St. John's, Newfoundland

Bedroom furnishings at Toronto's Black Creek Pioneer Village provide an essay in the wood turner's art.

Harbour Grace, Newfoundland

Merrick, Ontario

The classical lines of this house in Upper Canada Village attest to the Empire loyalist legacy in Ontario's building tradition.

Upper Canada Village ➞

Victorian baby carriage at the Colonel By Museum, Ottawa, Ontario

Springtime blossoms at the Hudson's Bay Company farm, Craigflower, on Vancouver Island

Centre gable over the entrance of this Ashton, Ontario house is a brief gothic gesture in the persistent Ontario Georgian style, not admitted to the more rigid formalism of the early nineteenth-century Harbour Grace house, Newfoundland.

Harbour Grace, Newfoundland

The dormered roof enclosing an upper floor typifies the late nineteenth-century mansard style. Charlottetown, P.E.I.

Bedroom, loyalist house, St. John, New Brunswick

Myrtleville child's cot, Brantford, Ontario

Runciman House, Annapolis Royal, Nova Scotia

Myrtleville, Brantford, Ontario →

The later nineteenth century, a prelude to our own modern times, was an age of ebullient enthusiasm for the machine, mass production, mechanical transportation, and the instant new wealth they created. Applied directly to the construction industry these translated into large-scale logging, quarrying, brickmaking and assembly-line milling and fabrication.

What first deceives the eye as meticulous craftsmanship, is often an agglomeration of mass-produced decorative detail. Such ostentatious ornamentation was not always accompanied by improved design or building quality. However, by the 1890s, expanses of patterned shingles, bargeboards fretted to intricate designs, and brackets larded with all manner of turned knobs, crestings, and spindles attested to the wealth and community status claimed by the occupant.

Detail of loyalist house, St. John, N.B.

Formal Georgian with imposing columned portico is symbolically appropriate for Lieutenant-Governor's House, Charlottetown, P.E.I.

High-style classicism of the colonial period is best exemplified in surviving public and offical structures. Here we find the spirit of the British "age of enlightenment" transferred to the colonies through rational building forms, themselves borrowed from ancient Greece and Rome. Rigidly symmetrical facades reflect similar internal spatial arrangements. Temple porticoes, complete with gable pediments and classical columns, recall the pomp and splendour of Imperial power. Proportions emphasizing the horizontal within a regular geometric massing are features of the Georgian classical revival.

The classical saltbox form, an upright gable-roof house with what appears to be an extension on the rear, owes its origin to seventeenth-century New England building traditions. The massive mortise-and-tenon framing technology goes back even further to English medieval methods of construction. The spare geometry of the form and flat unadorned wall surfaces are perhaps evocations of early puritan values. Brief references to the Renaissance or classical tradition were to be found in the symmetrical arrangement of façade windows about a central door, or, as in the St. Andrew's example, the *Palladian* first-floor windows and Georgian fanlight over the entrance.

A classical saltbox *at St. Andrews, N.B.*

Lunenberg, Nova Scotia

A room for withdrawing to, Myrtleville, Brantford, Ontario

A fanciful variation on the Victorian mansard style, Bluenose Lodge, Lunenberg, N.S. ➡

Brackets, finials, balusters, capitals, cresting, barge boards, fretwork, spindles, mouldings, stringcourses, all celebrated in a phrase, "the gaiety of gables", constitute the vocabulary of the Victorian builder. A shift in emphasis from craftsman and joiner to tradesman and machinist in the business of building is evident everywhere in nineteenth-century structures. Bought by the yard or by the dozen, in wood, tin, or cast iron, these elements could be applied in abundance to any basic house form. Indeed many older buildings were done over in the new manner, thus deceiving the modern eye as to their real age.

Whimsey and delight — a gingerbread detailing on a porch in North Gower, Ontario

High-style Victorian mansard with cast iron cresting renders a picturesque roofline, in Kingston, Ontario

Ornamental hardware, Craigdarroch Castle, Victoria, B.C.

Art Nouveau stained glass window, Craigdarroch Castle

Evidence of Victorian leisure-time activities at Point Ellice house, Victoria

The current run on "old oak", "pioneer pine", and "Quebec maple" decor, concurrent with the fashion for reproduction furniture in the "character home", bespeaks a revival of awareness in the trappings of personal life styles. Our manner of dress, the objects with which we surround our various activities, are the result of conscious or un-conscious decisions about our own self-image. Our tastes reflect our interests, education, economic well-being, perhaps even our travel experiences. In an historic house museum the period interior is a personal diary of the former occupant. Imported wallpapers indicate the facility and direction of transportation modes; finishings of exotic hardwoods and elaborate carvings might indicate considerable wealth and disposable income.

Conversely, the newspaper wall covering and hard-clay floors of the settler's cabin reveal the poverty and isolation of pioneer life. The family shrine, that common mantlepiece assemblage of ancestral and contemporary portraits, remains a more personal note common even in our times. Portraits of the Virgin or the King will denote definite religious or national affiliations. Since man first started building houses he has personalized them through use of decoration as a memorial in his own image.

Craigflower Manor china, Victoria, B.C.

A Craigdarroch Castle mantle, Victoria
Musical still life at the O'Keefe Ranch, Vernon, B.C. →

Under such rallying cries as "here today, gone tomorrow", or "this old house", the home restoration industry in Canada, over a short space of time, achieved astounding popularity. "Character homes" demand a premium in the real estate market. Pickers crowd demolition sites scavenging period hardware: panelled doors, Victorian mouldings, old porcelain bathroom fixtures, gilt faucet sets, brass door knobs, tongue-and-groove or old dimensional lumber, and Edwardian profile drop-siding. Craftsmen such as the mason, joiner, slatelayer and stained glass glazier, are in strong demand.

Yet there are pitfalls in even so laudable a pursuit as do-it-yourself restoration. Often in his enthusiasm the would-be old-house buyer does not foresee the intransigence of building code inspectors who still enforce modern regulations, unsympathetic to historic construction methods. Or, in the flurry of restoration, tradesmen and houseowner forget the fairly simple practice of recording work on the fabric by means of notes and photographs before, during and after restoration. This chapter in the building's history may go unrecorded for future owners. Before beginning work or even purchasing, many of the later trials and tribulations of the neophyte restorer can be avoided by a close and detailed inspection of the building fabric, from foundation drain tile to gable finial.

Attention to detail is the hallmark of good restoration practice.
◄—*A Victoria, B.C. character home*

Victorian parlour scene, Barkerville, B.C.

PRIVATE
PARKING
VIOLATERS WILL BE TOWED AWAY

2118

2120

The Second Empire style, characterized by the mansard roof enclosing the top storeys, is ultimately derived from sixteenth-century French palace architecture. The style became popular during the late nineteenth century, especially for hotels and public buildings throughout Europe and North America. St. John's, Newfoundland must be unique, however, in that a curious variant of this international style is the predominant mode in the historic townscape. The popularization of the mansard manner can be traced to the dominance of an early architectural firm which specialized in house design and construction during the late nineteenth century. J. and J. T. Southcott designs featured a concave mansard roof with hooded dormer windows, and bay windows on the ground floor. After St. John's disastrous fire of 1892, the so-called "Southcott style" characterized most of the new dwellings, both individual and row housing, of the extensive rebuilding program.

Individual by colour rather than form — row housing in St. John's, Newfoundland

←— *Halifax, Nova Scotia*

St. John's, Newfoundland

St. John's, Newfoundland

Modern planting complements old buildings in this contemporary courtyard St. John's, Newfoundland

49

Montreal, Quebec

Eclectic is a term commonly associated with late Victorian architecture. The depths of history and far-off climes were ransacked for exotic forms and unusual details. This reflected the internationalism of an age characterized by extensive travel, far-flung empires, and a popular interest in antiquarianism and new disciplines such as anthropology. The resulting range and variety of building styles allowed architectural symbolism to flourish as each building could be personalized according to the tastes of the builder. Fundamental to this new democracy of styles was mass-production technology. Everything from regular dimension timber and incised brass doorplates to complex granite moulding profiles and elaborate cast iron roof crestings could be mass produced. Range of style, size and quantity was limited only by the pocketbook. The standard house or the regular entrance door could, therefore, appear in the fancy dress of any number of elaborate disguises.

Gothic revival row housing in Montreal, Quebec

Baroque console brackets frame this doorway in Quebec City, Quebec.

One of the attractions of older buildings is the readability of their parts. The elements of the classical doorway — pediment, entablature, columns with capitals at the top, and a base or podium provided by the lower steps — are so traditional they are understood even by the contemporary untutored eye. First impressions have always been considered of paramount importance. A substantial door has been the pride of homeowners from cottages to castles.

A great poet once observed that we enter and leave this life through portals both physical and metaphoric. Indeed, the gate and door have been associated with ceremony. From the Roman triumphal arch and medieval city gates to the festive painted and carved house fronts of the West Coast Haidas, the door has proved a significant architectural symbol. Only in recent years has modern design practice downgraded the entry to the extent that, on many public buildings it is next to impossible to find!

We must demand a revival of the "doorway" in architecture.

Pediment and pillars make this entrance a miniature temple-front in Quebec City, Quebec

*L*ike first-settlement houses, the arrival of industry and commerce made do with buildings of a utilitarian scale and quality. However, as social rank and depth of purse were soon expressed in the size and quality of abode, so commerce was quick to adapt architecture to its self-promotion. Once basic function has been accommodated, the nineteenth century entrepreneur rarely stinted from joining the battle of ornament on mainstreet: indeed thus *mainstreet* was created.

The nineteenth century witnessed the urbanization of Canada and the growth of towns according to such middle-class principles as the separation of work and recreation and later on further divisions; industry, commerce, retailing, family life. Towns and cities in their development and planning began to segregate such activities with the creation of districts or zones for heavy manufacturing, retail activity, residential and open green space. Urban amenities could then be concentrated to support these functions. Formal parks such as Montreal's Westmount or Victoria's Beacon Hill were established. Winnipeg could create a warehouse district, Montreal the St. Jacques Street business sector, Halifax its arsenal. In Vancouver the wealthy could segregate themselves on Shaughnessy Heights, in Toronto within Rosedale.

This old stagecoach probably stopped regularly at the Hat Creek Ranch roadhouse now being restored near Cache Creek, British Columbia.

Despite vigorous settlement immigration within the last hundred years, Canada has experienced, like other countries of the western world, a population shift from country to town. Mechanization and the intensification of capital into larger farming units have resulted in a picturesque if somewhat melancholy feature to the landscape: bleak, abandoned farmsteads stand like silent ghosts beside caches of obsolete rusting machinery, the everpresent silver-grey fingers of broken cartwheels reach forlornly from the rustling grass. Across the country, from Saskatoon's Western Development Museum to Black Creek Pioneer Village, the age of steam and other nearly forgotten farming methods are celebrated by yearly ploughing or threshing *fêtes*.

Carlton, Ontario

The rehabilitation of mainstreet or "old town", is now a national enterprise. The rejuvenation of the commercial core, after years of strangulation by suburban growth, is now being addressed by all levels of government. Projects such as Vancouver's Gastown and Toronto's Yorkville demonstrate the extent to which local government is prepared to go in creating an ambience which will encourage people to return and businesses to stay. Services are improved, unsightly overhead wires buried, a "floorscape" with a period flavour, such as textured brick or quarried granite, is installed. Vehicular traffic is segregated from the pedestrian; "people-places" are created with benches and greenery in alleyways and squares defined by the historic structures themselves. Particular attention is paid to visual features. Paint schemes are controlled for period authenticity. Shop signs and street signs alike must also be low-key and sympathetic. The design of street bollards, lighting fixtures, even garbage cans, manhole covers, and telephone booths is closely monitored to support the period theme. As "downtown" again becomes a nice place to be, both commerce and its clientele are again attracted to enliven the streets. Crass consumerism can be couched in entertainment and delight.

Quebec City, Quebec

←*Bastion Square, Victoria, British Columbia, sparked the restoration program in that city during the 1960s.*

Restored mainstreet, Barkerville, British Columbia, where tourists have replaced gold seekers.

61

Vancouver's Gastown, where the historic structures have prompted a period re-creation.

In recent years, The Heritage Canada Foundation has played a catalytic role in urban conservation. Promoting the idea of "conservation areas" it has worked closely with government and the private sector to construct both a legal and economic framework for the conservation of the urban fabric. Conservation areas were established as demonstration projects, all different in scale and function: the Edwardian residential area of Strathcona in Edmonton; a warehouse and commercial district in the heart of Winnipeg; a Victorian port-side area integrating retail and residential row-housing in old St. John's, Newfoundland; and near the birthplace of Confederation, a small-scale residential district in Charlottetown, Prince Edward Island. With each project revolving funds were established to buy and recycle derelict or run-down structures. In

each case the effect was to create an economic climate and a physical model for the private developer or business owner to follow. The buyer had to agree to restrictions on the use of his property, alterations to the façade, and make a commitment to a high quality of building maintenance. In many cases the areas or individual structures are "designated." This means demolition is illegal without government sanction. Since inception the conservation area concept has meant commercial rejuvenation, rising property values for the home owner as the area becomes more desirable, and even improved tax revenue for government coffers.

Market Square, in Victoria, B.C. is a Heritage Canada award winner for conservation design excellence.

Black Creek Pioneer Village, Toronto, Ontario

A tinsmith at work in Upper Canada Village, Morrisburg, Ontario

64

There is a special magic in bringing to life the forgotten times concealed in historic buildings and their artifacts. Houses can be furnished with the tables, chairs, fabrics and wallpapers of their early history while maintaining the rudimentary forms of plumbing and lighting. Building restorations are often carried out using traditional tools and methods. Original settings and landscapes are often effected with plant species no longer in common use. Guides dressed in period costume greet the visitor. Old-time crafts and skills are demonstrated, from baking bread in a wood-burning stove to fabricating tin kettles.

The blacksmith and wheel wright ply their trades while explaining the processes to the visitor. Many sites offer "live-in' experiences for school children as an immersion course in local history. In Barkerville one can try a hand at panning for gold. The sensitivity to historical context gleaned through visits to historic sites enhances our appreciation of the remaining urban heritage where environment and use are now less sympathetic.

O'Dell Museum, Annapolis Royal, Nova Scotia.

The rehabilitation of historic structures, the rejuvenation of near abandoned civic cores, and the resulting return of commerce, residents and tourists to these areas, has reactivated a healthy and vigorous street life. A fresh breeze is blowing through old institutions — educational, entertaining, and profitable. The sidewalk cafe has reappeared from Victoria to Niagara-on-the-Lake where weary sightseers and shoppers can rest and watch the panoply of characters and events which make the street ongoing vaudeville. Street musicians and other buskers add zest and colour. In Kingston an old-time general store continues business in the traditional manner adding yet another service, tours for local school children. A community produce market is revived amid the old corrugated-iron industrial buildings of Vancouver's Granville Island, complete with surrounding marina, live theatre and an art school complex.

In places such as Kingston, Ottawa, or Toronto's St. Lawrence area, established markets experience a reawakening of public interest and commercial trade. The underlying principal to these events, for that is really what they are, is participation. More leisure time and movement away from such static occupations as television entertainment have turned a whole generation into community participants. Live theatre in playhouses such as Victoria's McPherson, a restored circuit vaudeville playhouse, or the nearby Belfry in a recycled Fernwood church, can be compared to the live entertainment in folk restaurants of Vieux Montréal.

Market Day behind Kingston's meticulously restored city hall

Ottawa, Ontario

School children dress up to relive pioneer life at Black Creek Village, Toronto.

Sidewalk cafes in Quebec City

Streetscapes in historic lower town, Quebec City

"From sea unto sea", the catch phrase of confederation was to call for a transcontinental railroad. Dubbed "the impossible dream" of Sir John A. MacDonald and the band of capitalists clustered about men such as Sir William Van Horne, the impact of the success is still deeply pressed into the fabric of this country. From a pedestrian brick roundhouse in Vancouver to the chateauesque pile of Quebec City station, the railroad spawned both monuments of individual splendor and entire towns with even greater ambitions. By 1890 Winnipeg, at the confluence of some twelve competing lines, American and Canadian, was labelling itself "the Gateway to the West".

The railway hotels such as Ottawa's Laurier and Quebec's Frontenac dressed up in the manner of French aristocratic hunting lodges and cavernous stations such at Toronto's Union, built to vie with the Roman Baths of Caracalla, have all been rallying points in the battle to preserve significant landmarks of Canadian architecture. But the transportation revolution, from train to automobile and airplane, has proven the downfall to the smaller but just as significant network of country stations which dot the country and provide a picturesque focal point of section towns such as Fernie, nestled in the Rockies' Crows Nest Pass. Small communities have begun to appreciate Canada's heritage of small stations, recycling them as day-care centres, museums, or tourist bureaus — just in time, it is thought by some, to preserve them for the travellers' eventual return to the railroad in the coming age of expensive fuel and congested freeways.

Edmonton railway station

Commercial streetscape, St. John, N.B.

The historic streetscape is a *mélange* of half-forgotten memories and nearly-remembered anecdotes gaining colour, verve and drama with each retelling. The buildings themselves stand as mute testimony to the rich folklore with which their past is embroidered. Yet the very secret of their popular attraction is not simply that they are symbols of one man's success, or a major event in the history of a community; it is that they invite the imagination to construct what is now only suggested by the worn façades, whimsical decorative detail, the patina of rust and peeling paint. Only in such museum environments as Barkerville or Upper Canada Village can the popular imagination be educated to fill in, with broad brushstrokes, the past life of a Canadian mainstreet. Yet every community can, by probing the oral record, searching out the lineage of land titles and street indexes, by combing archives, family albums and pictorial evidence, recreate the historical interlude. Today, walking tours with informed guides, interpretation centres, historic street maps and architectural guide books are proving popular with tourists, students, and citizens alike. Through diligent research old buildings can recapture their history.

Montreal, Quebec

The modern commercial strip has become a visual jungle of aggressive neon and searing day-glow colours. In certain historic areas signage is restricted, allowing the buildings to assert their individual character. A good shop sign respects the scale of the structure, is inspired by the historic period and the nature of the establishment, and is informative but visually restive.

Innovative signs with an historic flavour in Montreal

Testimonies to the skills of the ironworker and foundryman in Quebec City

These buildings in Charlottetown, P.E.I. await sensitive restoration.

The immigrant in search of a homestead, the itinerant peddlar and preacher on his circuit, the hungry gold-seeker trekking north, the farmer journeying to his distant market, or the Edwardian remittance-man-cum-tourist, are each the product of a vast land characterized by incredible distances. Serving a population continually on the move, hostelries and hotels have played an important role in Canadian life.

From the township roadhouses memorialized in the paintings of Cornelius Krieghoff to the crude hostelries of the Cariboo gold rush, here was an *en route* home, news centre, watering hole, and resting place distinguished not so much by the luxury of appointments but the reputation of its patron and occasionally, in urban centres, the cook. Almost irrespective of age and location, on the frontier or in the rural outback, the hostelry clung to the medieval traditions of its European ancestors; large barn-like structures were built clustered together to provide warmth and protection; men and animals shared the same or adjacent accommodation.

As the nineteenth-century town came of age, with its contiguous streetscapes and modern amenities, the hotels gained more respectability, distinguished by their balconied windows from which clientelle leisurely observed street life in the host town. Kings of this genre were, of course, the great railway hotels. In large towns the hotels were huge multi-storey edifices, dressed either in the classical finery of Renaissance palaces or with the turrets, spires, crenelations and massive roofscapes of Loire Valley chateaux.

In smaller towns, or, for example, stops of interest commanding magnificent views of the Rocky Mountains, hotels were mundane shingle-clad structures, sometimes in the manner of alpine *chalêts*. Whatever their form, for tourist or immigrant, they created a special and distinct image of this country which would inspire both memories of pleasure and visions of enterprise.

Interior of the restaurant now located in the home of actress Marie Dressler, born in Cobourg, Ontario, in 1868.

STRATHCONA HOTEL

Built by the Calgary and Edmonton Railway (later Canadian Pacific Railway), the Strathcona Hotel opened for business on December 5th, 1891. It is the oldest wood frame building in Strathcona. During prohibition the hotel became the Westminster Ladies College. This simply designed, but functional, building has offered rest and comfort to thousands of weary travellers.

EDMONTON HISTORICAL BOARD

Strathcona Hotel, Edmonton, Alberta

One process characteristic of urban life is change itself. Buildings, their functions and patterns of use, evolve with recurring cycles of new replacing old. Yet, a selection of structures must be held over, if only as landmarks in this process of growth and change. By noting where we come from these buildings help us remember who we are. The picturesque rooflines and ornamented portals of Victorian commercial architecture add diversity, even levity, to an urban fabric increasingly dominated by no-nonsense twentieth-century functionalism. Buildings such as Toronto's *Gooderham* are lessons in architecture. Within the architectural profession the tides of taste often call for a reshaping of past forms, even as the Victorians did in the last century. For the current vogue of architectural "post modernism" the *Gooderham* and its like stand as reference points.

The Gooderham flatiron building survives, crowded by the new towers of downtown Toronto.

A Heritage Canada mortgage will assist in recovering a useful commercial life for this Ottawa building.

Kingston, Ontario

84

As a home away from home the hostelry of old, along with its attendant functions — bar, restaurant and entertainment centre — has become a focus of heritage interest within the travel industry. While historic hotels such as Winipeg's old Fort Garry and Victoria's Empress are painstakingly restoring the Edwardian grandeur of their *decor,* at a popular level ersatz heritage interiors are being created with gay abandon, fueled by the wholesale looting of artifacts and architectural pieces for the purpose from Halifax to Prince Rupert. Banks, warehouses, even railway cars briefly submerge to reappear as "ye olde pubs", or "Cross Road Inns".

Wharfside buildings, Halifax, where restoration has re-created an exciting public waterfront

A Regina bank. The imposing classical dress only adds a note of melancholy to its isolated splendour as high-density construction closes in.

← *Montreal, Quebec*

If mainstreat became the focus for trade and commerce, the urban core soon became a battleground of styles and symbols in the interest of government services. Political aggrandizement and regional pride was inflated, or transgressed (according the size and elaboration of the structure) with the erection of public buildings. Classical provincial courthouses, vault-like land registries, and after the public education acts of the 1880s, large-scale school buildings began to dominate the landscape. In clergy-dominated Quebec the convent schools are the major landmarks in many communities. The *riposte* of the Dominion government consisted in the mansard-style post offices and custom houses scattered across the country, designed to echo the Second-Empire style parliament buildings in Ottawa.

From 1900 to 1914 the earlier severe Victorian essence of these buildings gave way to the more opulent Edwardian Beaux-Arts versions observable in such examples as the Granville and Hastings post office in Vancouver or the main post office in Ottawa. By the turn of the century the adornment of towns and cities had become a national obsession. Municipal governments happily raised taxes to provide grandiose monuments which disguised city halls, fire halls and libraries, the latter subsidized by the American capitalist and philanthropist Andrew Carnagie. The civic skyline achieved a recognizable character from coast to coast.

Iron fronts in downtown Toronto

Regina Post Office ⟶

Canadian Imperial Bank of Commerce (built 1910-12) centre, and Bank of Hamilton (built 1916), Winnipeg, Manitoba. One of Canada's most grand expressions of the Edwardian style.

Confederation Life Building (built 1912), a dramatic landmark on Winnipeg's Main Street, and last major office tower built in the grand Edwardian style

Also onto mainstreet crowded the financial institutions. Self-important in their columns, classical friezes and entablatures, they vied with government monuments for attention if not trade. Many were shaky structures, not designed for a long life, but nevertheless, by means of granite porticoes (simulated if not real) and luxuriously appointed interiors, a show of solidity and respectability was attempted. Most banks were classical in style, while some branches of the Bank of Montreal, banker to the Canadian Pacific Railroad, borrowed the chateau motifs of CP's stations and hotels. In major urban centres after 1900 these institutions manifested their presence through major structures of skyscraper proportions. Eminating from Montreal's financial district, where most banks and life insurance companies, indeed the stock exchange itself, had their headquarters, these massive overblown Greek temples and renaissance palaces began to dominate the civic cores of Halifax, Toronto, Winnipeg, Calgary and Vancouver alike.

Such building continued into the 1920s with department store chains such as the Hudsons Bay Company and Timothy Eaton's building their own gleaming *terra-cotta* emporiums. Individually and together they challenged even such major monuments as provincial parliament buildings in size and luxury.

Unlike the soaring glass monoliths of contemporary design these first proud towers were sheathed in ornament. Mass-produced *terra-cotta* and cast iron, or machine-dressed stone, was fashioned into myriad images to deceive and delight the eye. At street level, massive rusticated masonry blocks appear to effortlessly support the towering structure above. Huge piers or heavy columns frame imposing entrance porticoes; above this soar fluted columns often linked by embossed brass spandrels or classical entablature-like skirts.

Rooflines were accentuated by a massive parapet, sometimes precariously supported by intricately carved brackets or reverse-curved consoles. Tucked into shadows any hint of previous restraint gives way to a riot of entwined foliage, swagged festoons, even grimacing gargoyls, sensuously lithe caryatides or complex escutcheons, all primly framed with staid classical egg-and-dart mouldings. Of course, all this was architectural legerdemaine; these aesthetically contrived skins masked heavy steel skeletons webbed with conduit and service shafts which made them more machine than structure. Yet, intended as an artistic feat for the newfound urbanite, these ecclectic constructs of the draughtsman's pen continue to intrigue and amuse even the most casual onlooker.

Coburg, Ontario Town Hall →

Fanciful renaissance detailing creates a 'layercake' skin which masks the steel skeleton of the Paris Building (built 1915-25), Winnipeg, Manitoba.

Yates Street moulding, Victoria, B.C.

← *Lindsay Building, Winnipeg, Manitoba*

Spaghetti Foundry (restaurant), Victoria, B.C.

Even today nationhood finds ultimate monumental expression at the seat of government. Architectural conceit reflects the egotism of parliamentary power but in a way which expresses the special communal identity of the popular political will.

The Dominion's original parliament buildings in Ottawa, combining picturesque elements of the English gothic revival with the mansard roofline of the French Second-Empire style, symbolized the ancestral roots of nationhood, Westminster and Paris. Designed by architects Thomas Fuller and Chilian Jones and constructed between 1859 and 1866, the buildings, except the library, were destroyed by fire in 1916. Pearson and Marchand designed the replacement structure as we see it today, in much the same idiom.

Phenomenal urban growth as well as political enfranchisement across the country in the late nineteenth century, then in the midwest in the early years of the twentieth, prompted massive expenditures on "seats of government". But as with those of the Dominion, provincial structures were designed not only to house expanding government services and administrative programs but to serve as visual metaphors of regional pride and prosperity. Thus dawns the age of provincial legislative building with Quebec City's magnificently-sited French Renaissance range, completed in 1880. Others followed, inspired more perhaps by the classical styles of the then-abuilding American state capitols.

New Brunswick started construction of its legislative building at Fredericton in 1880. Ontario built its Queens Park Richardsonian-Romanesque pile in 1886; British Columbia's ambitious Romanesque-revival range was begun at Victoria in 1893. In 1905 the provinces of Alberta and Saskatchewan were created and building programs soon initiated: Alberta at Edmonton with a formal Beaux-Arts plan in 1907 and another in the same style by Saskatchewan at Regina in 1908, distinguished by its setting in a landscaped park complete with artificial lake. Manitoba, enjoying massive expansion through the territorial reorganizations of 1881 and 1912 began what is probably the most sumptuous expression of Edwardian Beaux-Arts imperial splendour in 1912 at Winnipeg.

Only Nova Scotia and Prince Edward Island have been content to live with their former legislative structures, both constructed in the first half of the nineteenth century.

Federal Parliament Buildings, Ottawa, Ontario

Gas lamp outside the York Town Hall, Toronto, Ontario

York Town Hall, Toronto →

Coburg, Ontario Town Hall

Restored City Hall (built 1878-91), Victoria, British Columbia

City Hall, Kingston (built 1844). A careful exterior restoration with an interior sensitively blending new furnishings with old decor.

103

Kingston, Ontario

Province House, Charlottetown, P.E.I. (built 1811-19). The birthplace of Confederation.

Federal Parliament Buildings, Ottawa, Ontario →

The Golden Boy, Legislative Buildings, Winnipeg, Manitoba

Legislative Buildings, Regina, Saskatchewan. A singular symbol of civilization on the prairie landscape.

Edmonton, Alberta Legislative Buildings ➜

The legislative program of post-Confederation Canada was much more than an expression of political aggrandizement and regional pride. Together, and in their localities, these structures established new standards in both the scale and quality of construction. Architectural competitions in New Brunswick, British Columbia, Saskatchewan and Manitoba attracted competitors world-wide. Tradesmen with specialized skills were drawn to the building projects and stayed on to practise their crafts in the region. Internal decorations were of an order and quality requiring the importation of technology, materials and products from the major fashion centres of the world. In many instances, therefore, the very construction of the buildings created small booms within the local economies.

Legislative Buildings, Edmonton

Legislative Buildings, Winnipeg, Manitoba

109

Restoration programs now ongoing in
Canada's major public buildings from
Ottawa's East Block to Charlottetown's Province
House and Victoria's Parliament Buildings have
provided an important training ground for
architectural preservation. The call has gone out
for many nearly dormant skills: glass painters,
tinsmiths, ornamental plasterers and stone
masons. Apprenticeships in these arts have been
re-established; new methods for re-engineering
and servicing these monolithic structures have
been developed. Original architectural integrity
has been preserved and enhanced. The spin-off,
both in trade skills and conservation technology,
has been the application of this experience in
courthouse, church and large commercial
restoration projects throughout the country.

Connaught Library (built 1912-16), Legislative Buildings, Victoria, British Columbia

Restored Jubilee Window, Legislative Buildings, Victoria ⟶

SPLENDOR SINE OCCASU

TO COMMEMORATE THE 60TH YEAR

OF THE REIGN OF QUEEN VICTORIA

1837

1897

Even today, in the age of anonymous towering highrises, the civic skyline would be incomplete without its complement of towers and spires — the mark of its churches, chapels, convents and synagogues. Quebec retained, well into the twentieth century, its massive Italian Baroque church-type. These remain large capacious buildings in the shadows of which huddle the small towns of rural Quebec. Upper Canada and the eastern Maritimes followed a different building tradition. The severe English-American classicism of the eighteenth century, in church architecture distinguished by its Gibsonian tower and classical portico, only very slowly admitted the influence of the nineteenth century Gothic revival. The so-called "hyperborean gothic" which distinguished a few mid-century East Coast Anglican churches by a peculiar adaptation to wood technology would find its stylistic progeny gracing the British

Columbia wilderness rather than uprooting the staid classical tradition of eastern Canada. Despite this, influential British gothicists made major contributions to Canadian church architecture. William Butterfield supplied designs for Christchurch Cathedral in Fredericton. George Gilbert Scott provided plans for St. John Cathedral at St. John's, Newfoundland. These structures, along with J. C.M. Keith's Christ Church Cathedral rising magnificently atop Church Hill in Victoria, stand as ecclesiastical book-ends to the continent and come closest to recapturing the desired effect of the old cathedral towns of Europe.

St. Eugene, Cranbrook, B.C.

Montreal, Quebec

Churchyard and church, Harbour Grace, Newfoundland

Mission church of St. Ann's (built ca. 1890) at O'Keefe Ranch, Vernon, B.C.

William Knox Church, Edmonton, Alberta

Gothic style church, St. Andrews, New Brunswick

St. George's "Little Dutch Church", (built 1756), Halifax, Nova Scotia. A historical monument which stands ➔
stubbornly resisting the encroachment of highrise suburbia.

Beyond this, and particularly on the western frontier while banks aspired to be temples of capital and enterprise, churches fast became monuments to entrepreneurial missionary zeal. Starting in the 1860s English Anglicans and French-Canadian Catholics built mission outposts throughout the western wilderness, for both white settlers and native peoples. In British Columbia townsites surveyed by the Royal Engineers featured a central or prominent "church reserve" for the Church of England. Methodists, Catholics, Presbyterians and others established where they could and all, initially, shared variations on the crude carpenter-gothic style. Other church-types have followed ethnic predilections. Jewish settlers seem to have preferred the round-arched Romanesque while, in the midwest, Ukrainians constructed central-plan structures with onion domes and free-standing bell towers, following established old-world traditions. Increasingly today these structures are threatened by population movements, and even by the growth and theological adaptions of the congregations themselves. Only the inherent conservatism of most religious persuasion has preserved this unique, if fragile, heritage.

Harbour Grace, Newfoundland

← *St. John's Church, Lunenberg, (built ca. 1840). One of the first examples of the*

Our built heritage, notwithstanding its substance, is fragile and threatened. Various agencies dedicated to its preservation need continual support. Parks Canada, operating as an arm of the federal government, maintains and commemorates sites of national significance and is advised by knowledgeable citizens through the Historic National Sites and Monuments Board. Lands and buildings can be designated for preservation in perpetuity either at the provincial or municipal levels. Both operate historic sites and interpretive "heritage parks" across the country. Recently some provinces have established heritage trusts or foundations to receive charitable donations and to financially support building conservation projects. Hundreds of small historical societies operate historic house museums and they are complemented by dozens of civic heritage amenity groups who educate and lobby local government in conservation matters. Thousands of home owners and businessmen have bought historic structures in which to live and work and are restoring them with dedication and care.

The Heritage Canada Foundation exists to assist the conservation movement at all levels. Its education program aims at training professionals and tradesmen in restoration skills. Its research resources assist government at all levels in devising protective legislation. The Heritage Canada Magazine, technical publications and films promote awareness and communication among conservation groups. Regional councils across the country organize annual meetings and seminars. The investment and mainstreet programs concentrate on assisting in the rejuvenation of decaying cores in historic small towns.

The preservation of Canada's built heritage is a success story of individuals and communities from sea to sea.

Upper Canada Village, Morrisburg, Ontario →

Quebec City

The Basilica, St. John's Newfoundland. A signal landmark dominating the town and harbour.

← *Notre Dame Cathedral, Montreal, Quebec (built 1823-9). The most sumptuous celebration of the gothic revival in Canada.*

123

Barkerville, B.C. cemetery

This book stems from my love and respect for some tenacious and proud survivors of Canada's fine architectural heritage. My work also expresses concern for a disappearing quality of life which these buildings represent and serves as a protest against much modern design — its insensitivity and inhumanity. Good design can match the new and old.

I have chosen to illustrate the architecture against the bright cheerfulness of Canada's lovely springs, sunny summers and colourful autumns. May we, just this once, forget winter? Otherwise, no special effects have been employed. The recorded scenes are presented as they are today. The equipment used has been the best obtainable: Linhof and Nikon cameras, Schneider Super Angulon lenses, Ilford black and white film and Kodak professional colour materials.

I would like to express my thanks to the many good people, dedicated to the cause of heritage preservation, who have helped me so much in my work, and special thanks to Mary Ann Baxter for her kind and generous encouragement. Also, my grateful appreciation is extended for the assistance given by the Canada Council, the Heritage Canada Foundation and the B.C. Heritage Trust. Finally, I must thank my wife, Margaret, without whose support my work would not be possible.

Philip F. Graham

Phototypography by
Professional Typesetting,
Victoria, British Columbia
in 11 point ITC Garamond type.